Musicians of the World:
Abida Parveen

By Shirin Lutfaeli

Library For All Ltd.

LIBRARY
FOR ALL

Library For All is an Australian not for profit organisation with a mission to make knowledge accessible to all via an innovative digital library solution. Visit us at libraryforall.org

Musicians of the World: Abida Parveen

This edition published 2022

Published by Library For All Ltd
Email: info@libraryforall.org
URL: libraryforall.org

Library For All gratefully acknowledges the contributions of all who made previous editions of this book possible.

This book was made possible by the generous support of Save The Children.

Save the Children

Original illustrations by Name of the Public Domain images & Creative Commons Licensed Images

Musicians of the World: Abida Parveen
Lutfaeli, Shirin
ISBN: 978-1-922827-96-8
SKU02699

Musicians of the World:
Abida Parveen

Abida Parveen is a famous Pakistani musician. She was born in Larkana in Sindh Province on 20 February 1954. Can you figure out how old Abida is now?

Here is a map of Pakistan, Abida's home country. Where is Sindh province? What are some of the countries next to Pakistan?

Early Life

Abida's father was also a musician. He had a music school in their hometown where he only used to tutor boys. Girls were not allowed to sing. But, because of Abida's talents, he decided to train her at his school. Abida sang her first solo song when she was just three years old.

Becoming a Musician
Abida was trained by her father to
sing in her native language of Sindhi.
But she also sings in other languages:
Urdu, Hindi, Punjabi, Seraiki, and
Persian. She and her father used to
practise her singing at shrines and
festivals around Pakistan. Abida was
very close to her father.

Abida writes some of own songs; she also sings songs written by other artists. She especially likes to sing traditional Pakistani folk songs and poems written by famous Pakistani and Indian poets. She is most famous for singing *ghazals*, a type of poem.

11

Abida Today

Abida is recognised as one of the most important singers of Pakistani *ghazals*. She has received many awards and has performed all over the world. She lives in Pakistan and has two daughters and a son.

Glossary

Award: to receive recognition for doing something well.

Festival: a day of celebration.

Native: related to the place of one's birth or origin.

Solo: to do something by one's self.

Shrine: a holy or sacred place dedicated to a religious figure.

Talent: having a skill or ability in something.

You can use these questions to talk about this book with your family, friends and teachers.

What did you learn from this book?

Describe this book in one word. Funny? Scary? Colourful? Interesting?

How did this book make you feel when you finished reading it?

What was your favourite part of this book?

download our reader app
getlibraryforall.org

About the contributors

Library For All works with authors and illustrators from around the world to develop diverse, relevant, high quality stories for young readers. Visit libraryforall.org for the latest news on writers' workshop events, submission guidelines and other creative opportunities.

Did you enjoy this book?

We have hundreds more expertly curated original stories to choose from.

We work in partnership with authors, educators, cultural advisors, governments and NGOs to bring the joy of reading to children everywhere.

Did you know?

We create global impact in these fields by embracing the United Nations Sustainable Development Goals.

libraryforall.org

*9 7 8 1 9 2 2 8 2 7 9 6 8 *